THE OLYMPICS HISTORY

THE OLYMPICS HISTORY

Moira Butterfield

SEA-TO-SEA
Mankato Collingwood London

This edition first published in 2012 by

Sea-to-Sea Publications
Distributed by Black Rabbit Books
P.O. Box 3263, Mankato, Minnesota 56002

Printed in United States of America, North Mankato, MN

9 8 7 6 5 4 3

Published by arrangement with the Watts
Publishing Group Ltd, London.

Library of Congress Cataloging-in-Publication Data

Butterfield, Moira, 1960-
The Olympics: History / by Moira Butterfield.
p. cm. -- (The Olympics)
Includes index.
ISBN 978-1-59771-319-1 (library binding)
1. Olympics--History--Juvenile literature. I. Title.
GV721.53.B88 2010
796.48--dc22
2011006470

Series editor: Sarah Ridley
Editor in chief: John C. Miles
Designer: Jason Billin
Art director: Jonathan Hair
Picture research: Diana Morris

Picture credits: Picture credits: Ace Stock/Alamy: 6bl. Arup/Rex Features: 27. BCMF Arquitectos: 29. Bettmann/Corbis: 17b, 18br. Adrian Dennis/AFP/Getty Images: 28c. Mary Evans PL: 9. Getty Images: 8b, 11t, 12. John Gichigi/Getty Images: 26. The Granger Collection/Topfoto: 13bl, 17t, 18bl. Hulton Archive/Getty Images: 10. Hulton-Deutsch/Corbis: front cover. Impact/Alamy: 6b. Jacques Langevin/Sygma/Corbis: 24. Library of Congress: 8t. LOCOG: 28b. mary416/Shutterstock: 25. Wally McNamee/Corbis: 23t. Gianni d'agli Orti/Museo Nazionale Terme, Roma/Art Archive: 7. Picturepoint/Topham: 14t, 14b, 15. Mike Powell/Getty Images: 22. Gerard Ranciman, Jean Guichard/Sygma/Corbis: 20. Jean-Yves Ruszniewski /TempSport/ Corbis: 5, 23b. Sports Illustrated/Getty Images: 21t, 21b. Topfoto: 3, 11b, 19. ullsteinbild/Topfoto: 13r. World History Archive/Topfoto: 16.

November 2011
RD/9781597712910/002

Note to parents and teachers

Every effort has been made by the Publishers to ensure that the web sites in this book are suitable for children, that they are of the highest educational value, and that they contain no inappropriate or offensive material. However, because of the nature of the Internet, it is impossible to guarantee that the contents of these sites will not be altered. We strongly advise that Internet access is supervised by a responsible adult.

CONTENTS

THE BIRTH OF THE OLYMPICS

The first recorded Olympic Games took place in 776 B.C.E., at Olympia in ancient Greece. Like the modern Olympics, they were held every four years. They continued for 1,100 years until 393 C.E.

The ancient Greeks believed that competitive sports pleased their gods, so they held the Games on a sacred temple site. At the opening ceremony, they lit a flame at the altar of Zeus, king of the Gods, and kept it burning until the Games ended. In the earliest Olympics, there was only one event—the "stadion," a sprint of almost 220 yards (about 200 m). A crowd up to 40,000-strong watched from the stadium.

An ancient Greek vase showing Olympic wrestlers.

The remains of the running track at Olympia, including stone starting blocks for the athletes.

Amazing Olympics

If any athlete was discovered to have cheated at the ancient Olympics, they were disqualified, whipped, and had to pay a fine that was used to pay for a statue of Zeus.

The Athletes

Ancient Greece was divided into separate city-states. Athletes represented their own city-state, called a polis. Eventually, competitors came from other parts of Europe and North Africa, too. The winners won a laurel wreath and a palm frond. Back home they were treated like celebrities and given valuable bonuses, such as free food. The main Olympics were for male athletes only, and women had their own separate event.

The Events

Gradually there were more events, such as boxing, wrestling, and a violent mixture of the two called the "pankration." More sprint races were added along with chariot-racing, long jump, and discus and javelin throwing. As well as the sports, there was an artistic side to the Games. Sculptors and poets carved statues of the star athletes or wrote poetry about them.

An ancient statue showing an Olympic discus thrower. All athletes competed naked at the Games.

Olympic Facts and Stats

First recorded champion Koroibos, a Greek cook, was the first recorded winner of the stadion race.

Most successful champion The runner Leonidas of Rhodes, who won 12 times between 164 B.C.E. and 152 B.C.E.

Most famous celebrity Wrestler Milon of Kroton (in southern Italy), who won six times between 540 B.C.E. and 516 B.C.E. He was a great showman who once carried a bull into the Olympic arena.

First female champion Kyniska of Sparta was declared winner of chariot races in 396 B.C.E. and 392 B.C.E., even though she was the team owner and trainer and didn't take part herself.

OLYMPICS REBORN

The Olympics were revived in 1896 through the efforts of Frenchman Baron Pierre de Coubertin.

At first, Baron de Coubertin found it difficult to get the Games going again, but he persevered and the first modern Olympics were held in Athens, Greece, in 1896. There were 43 events, including some unusual ones such as one-handed weightlifting and a swimming race only open to members of the Greek Navy. There were 245 competitors, all of them men, from 14 countries.

Setting Up the IOC

Baron de Coubertin set up the International Olympic Committee (IOC for short), which still sets the rules and organizes the Summer and Winter Olympics today. Its members come from the National Olympic Committees of the countries taking part, and between them they decide where the Olympics will be held.

▲ Baron de Coubertin (1863–1937)

▼ Crowds cheer Greek hero Spiridon Louis as he wins the marathon in Athens, Greece, in 1896.

The start of the first modern Olympic race ever, a heat for the 100-meter event in Athens, Greece, in 1896.

Moving On

The next two Olympic Games were held in France in 1900 and the USA in 1904. Women took part for the first time in 1900, where there were more surprising events, such as the equestrian (horse) high jump and a swimming obstacle race where competitors had to climb poles and swim under boats.

Amazing Olympics

In the first Olympic Games, the winners got a silver medal and the runners-up received a bronze. In the second Olympic Games, they all received trophies instead. Gold, silver, and bronze medals were first awarded at the third Games.

Olympic Facts and Stats

1896 The first modern Olympic Games were held in Athens, Greece.

1900 The first female Olympic champion, Charlotte Cooper of Great Britain, won the women's tennis event at the Paris Olympics.

1904 The first Africans to compete in the Olympics ran in the marathon event in St. Louis, Missouri. They were Tswana tribesmen who had been taking part in an exhibition nearby.

1904 American gymnast George Eyser won three gold medals, two silvers, and a bronze, despite having a wooden leg.

FASTER, HIGHER, STRONGER

From 1908 to 1928, the Olympics became more organized, and many more countries took part. The first Winter Olympics were held in Chamonix, France, in 1924.

Gradually, the Olympics gained features that are still used today. In 1908, the athletes marched into the stadium for the first time, nation by nation, and in 1912, electronic timing was introduced. At the Antwerp Games in 1920, the Olympic flag was flown, with five rings representing the continents from which the athletes are drawn: Africa, the Americas, Europe, Asia, and Oceania. The white background symbolizes peace.

Amazing Olympics

At the 1912 Games in Stockholm, Sweden, the longest-ever Olympic cycling race took place over 200 miles (320 km). The winner finished in just under 11 hours.

The Norwegian team parade behind their national flag at the 1908 Opening Ceremony in London.

Taking the Oath

An athlete took the Olympic Oath for the first time in 1920, something that still happens at the beginning of every Olympic Games. One chosen competitor repeats the oath on behalf of every athlete taking part.

The Olympic Motto

The IOC introduced an Olympic motto in 1924: "Citius, Altius, Fortius," which means "Higher, Faster, Stronger." It also introduced the Olympic Creed, which explains the ideals behind the Games:

"The most important thing in the Olympic Games is not to win but to take part, just as the most important thing in life is not the triumph, but the struggle. The essential thing is not to have conquered, but to have fought well."

In 1920, Belgian Victor Boin became the first athlete ever to take the Olympic Oath.

A female competitor in the shot put.

Olympic Facts and Stats

1908 The first brother and sister medalists, Willy and Lottie Dod of Great Britain, won archery medals.

1920 The oldest Olympic competitor ever, Swede Oscar Swahn, won a silver medal in a deer-shooting competition, aged 72.

1920 The tug-of-war appeared as an event in the Olympics for the last time.

1928 Women were allowed to compete in gymnastics and track and field events for the first time.

HARD TIMES AND HEROES

World War II (1939–45) overshadowed the Olympics between 1932 and 1948. Despite this, sports heroes and new innovations made the Games a better show.

In 1932, at the Los Angeles Games, the male athletes stayed in their own Olympic Village for the first time. The female athletes stayed in a luxurious hotel. Living quarters were not as comfortable at the London Games in 1948 because the UK was recovering from World War II. Athletes stayed in Royal Air Force camps, in schools, and in colleges. Today, specially designed Olympic Villages are always built for the Games.

Hitler's Games

In 1936, the Olympic Games were held in Berlin, Germany. The Nazi leader, Adolf Hitler, tried to use the Olympics to showcase his Nazi Party and particularly his racist views that Aryans—white-skinned Germans—were superior in every way to other peoples. The African-American sprinter and long-jumper, Jesse Owens, proved him spectacularly wrong by winning five gold medals.

Nazi swastikas decorated the stadium at the 1936 Olympics in Berlin, Germany.

Amazing Olympics

Hollywood movie stars, such as Marlene Dietrich, Gary Cooper, and Charlie Chaplin, entertained the crowds at the 1932 Games in Los Angeles.

Olympic Facts and Stats

1932 This was the first Games to take place over 16 days. Previous Olympics had been spread over four or five months.

1932 Sprinter Liu Changchun became the first Chinese competitor in the Olympics.

1936 All athletes were supposed to shout "Sieg Heil" (a Nazi slogan) and salute as they passed Adolf Hitler at the opening ceremony. Those who didn't were booed.

1940/1944 These Games were canceled because of World War II.

1948 U.S. sprinter Audrey Patterson became the first African-American woman to become an Olympic medalist.

Carrying the Flame

At the Berlin Games in 1936, the Olympic flame was carried by relay from Olympia in Greece to the Olympic stadium for the first time. Over the years, the flame has been carried in many different ways, including on a boat, on an airplane, on horseback, and by dog sled.

An athlete carries the Olympic torch for the first time in 1936. It was taken by relay from Olympia, in Greece, to Berlin, in Germany.

A poster for the 1948 London Olympics, showing the Houses of Parliament.

COLD WAR OLYMPICS

As TV and radio coverage grew, the Olympics became more and more popular. However, during the 1950s, they were affected by the Cold War—hostility and suspicion between the communist countries of the Soviet Union and the democratic countries of Western Europe and the United States.

At the 1952 Helsinki Games the Soviet Union entered the competition for the first time. Their athletes had followed very focused training programs and came away with many medals. Sports became a

Czech long-distance runner Emile Zatopek won three golds at the 1952 Olympics.

The opening ceremony in Melbourne, Australia, in 1956. Photography was still black and white.

sort of fake war between democratic and communist countries, and sports triumphs were seen as symbols of the success of either side. Some athletes from communist countries defected, refusing to go home after the Games and asking for political asylum in the West.

Amazing Olympics

Every Olympic Games has an official number and the title "Olympiad." For instance, the 2012 London Games will be the Thirtieth Olympiad (XXX in Roman numerals).

Protestors and Boycotts

The Games became the focus for protests and boycotts, because they gave protestors a chance to gain worldwide publicity. Arab countries withdrew from the 1956 Summer Olympics in protest at Israeli military actions, while some European countries refused to take part in protest at the Soviet invasion of Hungary.

A New Closing Ceremony

In 1956, the closing ceremony changed. Instead of marching into the stadium country by country, all the athletes came in together, to show friendship and unity. This continues today.

The water polo final in 1956 descended into a fistfight between the Hungarian and Soviet teams as tensions flared after the Soviet invasion of Hungary in 1956.

Olympic Facts and Stats

1952 Lisa Hartel of Denmark won a silver medal in a riding event despite being paralyzed below the knee by polio. She was helped on and off her horse to compete.

1956 The Games in Melbourne, Australia, were the first to be held in the Southern Hemisphere.

1956 During the Melbourne Games, the horse events had to be held in Stockholm, Sweden, because animal quarantine laws prevented horses from entering Australia.

1956 American weightlifter Charles Vinci was over the weight limit for his event, but managed to qualify by cutting off his hair at the very last minute to lose 7 ounces (200 g).

SPORTING SIXTIES

During the 1960s, politics continued to cause trouble at the Olympics. However, the Games grew in size and, in 1960, the first Paralympic Games were held a few weeks after the Summer Games.

Politics began to play a big part in the Olympic story. During the 1968 Olympics in Mexico City, two African-American sprinters staged a silent protest for black civil rights during the medal ceremony for the 200-meter sprint. They were promptly banned from the Games and from Mexico. Meanwhile South Africa was banned from the Olympics because of its racist government policy of Apartheid, which segregated black and white South Africans (kept them separate in schools, jobs, and towns).

Drugs Testing and Sports Science

The first drugs disqualification occurred in 1968 after a Swedish athlete tested positive for having too much alcohol in his blood. Sports science was still very underdeveloped compared to modern times.

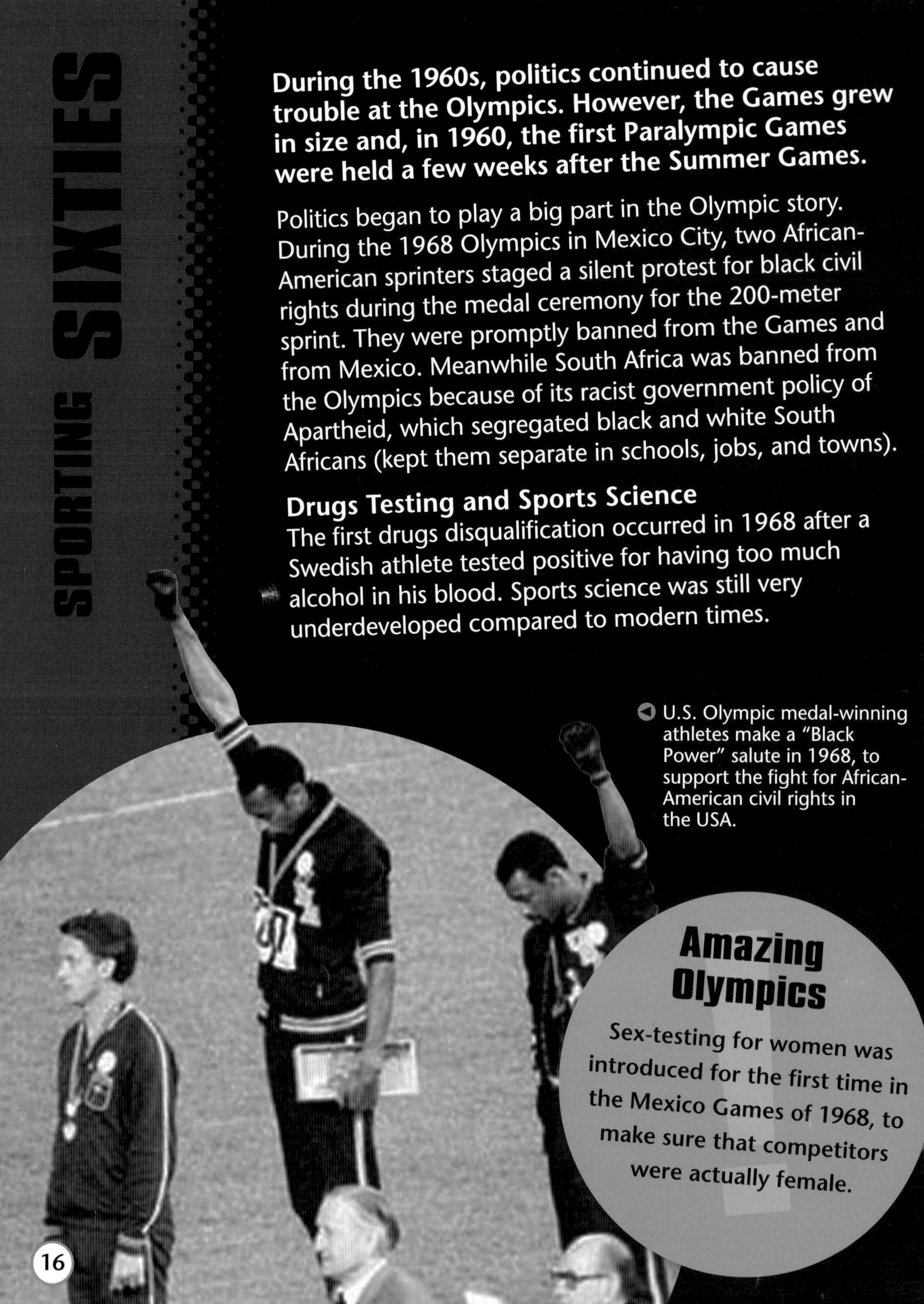

U.S. Olympic medal-winning athletes make a "Black Power" salute in 1968, to support the fight for African-American civil rights in the USA.

Amazing Olympics

Sex-testing for women was introduced for the first time in the Mexico Games of 1968, to make sure that competitors were actually female.

Olympic Facts and Stats

1960 During the Rome Olympics, some events were held on ancient Roman sites, such as the 2,000-year-old site of a wrestling ring.

1964 The Tokyo Olympics were the first to be held in Asia.

1964 The first Olympic wedding took place when two Bulgarian athletes got married in the Tokyo Olympic Village.

1964 Abebe Bikila of Ethiopia won the marathon just six weeks after having his appendix out.

For instance, nowadays athletes have a carefully structured scientific training program to help them deal with hot conditions. In 1960, however, British walker Don Thompson prepared for the heat of Rome in summer by training in a bathroom full of heaters and boiling kettles.

TV and Broadcasting Revenue

The Olympics were shown in color on TV for the first time in the 1960s. The new technology meant that the IOC could begin to sell broadcasting rights to TV companies around the world. At first, they charged a few hundred thousand dollars, but in 2012, the sale of the broadcasting rights for the London Summer Olympics is expected to earn the IOC more than $3 billion.

A poster for the 1960 Rome Olympics.

An exhausted athlete in Mexico City, 1968. Because Mexico City is located at a high altitude, there is less oxygen in the air than normal, making running extra tough.

TRIUMPHS AND DISASTER

In the 1970s, the Olympics saw tragedy, but also celebrated extraordinary performances that captivated TV audiences around the world.

Tragedy and violence hit the 1972 Munich Olympics when Palestinian terrorists broke into the Olympic Village and took members of the Israeli team hostage. Eleven Israeli team members, five terrorists, and a policeman died, and the Olympics were suspended until the IOC decided to go on with the Games. Ever since this incident, security has become much tighter at international sports events.

Screen Fame

Despite troubles off the track, the Olympic sports triumphs of the 1970s were enjoyed by millions of people because home TVs had become much more common. Among the athletes who became household names were American swimmer Mark Spitz and Russian gymnast Olga Korbut. Then in 1976, Romanian gymnast Nadia Comãneci won the first perfect gymnastics score ever—10.00.

▲ Gymnast Olga Korbut won four golds and two silvers in 1972 and 1976.

◄ Swimmer Mark Spitz won seven golds in Munich, Germany, in 1972.

Early Paralympic athletes take part in a basketball game.

The Paralympics

Until 1976, only wheelchair competitors could take part in the Paralympics, but now the IOC changed its rules to allow other disabilities, too. In 1976, disabled skiers competed in the first Paralympic Winter Olympics in Sweden. Now thousands of disabled athletes compete in all kinds of summer and winter Olympic sports.

Amazing Olympics

The 1972 Munich Olympics had the first cartoon mascot—Waldi the dachshund. Now every Olympic Games has an official mascot.

Olympic Facts and Stats

1972 British horse Cornishman V appeared in Hollywood movies as well as helping his riders win two gold medals.

1972 A German student disguised as an athlete joined the marathon race near the end and pretended to be the winner. The real winner arrived a few minutes later.

1976 Japanese gymnast Shun Fujimoto continued competing with a broken kneecap, gritting his teeth and not telling anyone, to help his team win gold.

1976 The Winter Games were awarded to Denver, Colorado, but residents voted against paying for it, so the Games had to move to Innsbruck, Austria.

TV TIMES

In the 1980s, business sponsors began to invest in the Olympics, buying the right to get their products displayed and advertised during the event. The organizers of the Olympics needed the money because the cost of staging the Games now ran into billions.

Although Olympic athletes were supposed to be amateur (earning no money from their sport), communist countries supported their athletes full-time, so they didn't need other jobs and had a lot more time to train. This forced the IOC to change the rules in 1988 to enable most Olympic athletes to be professionals. They were allowed to get sponsorship—regular money—from businesses such as sports equipment manufacturers, and were given permission to endorse and advertise products.

▼ The 1984 Los Angeles Olympics was the first privately funded Olympic Games, supported by businesses and sponsorship deals.

Ben Johnson hit the headlines for taking drugs. He was stripped of his gold medal.

Illegal Drugs and More Boycotts

Soon the IOC was dealing with a different type of problem—illegal drugs. In 1988, Ben Johnson, Olympic 100-meter sprint champion, became the most famous athlete at the time to test positive for a performance-enhancing drug and he was stripped of his medal. Added to this, the Olympics were affected by politics again. Countries led by the United States pulled out of the 1980 Games to protest against the Soviet invasion of Afghanistan, and in 1984, the Soviets organized their own boycott in revenge.

Opening Ceremony

The Opening Ceremony at the 1984 Los Angeles Olympics was a huge theatrical show. Five giant Olympic rings were lit, there were rock stars, performers, and a rocket man who flew into the stadium. Since then opening ceremonies have become a massive event watched by millions worldwide.

Amazing Olympics

At every Olympic Games, new sports are added and old ones are dropped. At the 1984 Olympics, synchronized swimming appeared for the first time.

In 1984, synchronized swimming became an Olympic sport, with team and individual events.

Olympic Facts and Stats

1984 McDonald's paid $4 million to have the Olympic swimming pool named after the company.

1984 Women ran the marathon for the first time. Decades before, doctors had banned women from running long distances in case they "became old too soon."

1988 At the Calgary Winter Olympics, the Jamaican bobsled team appeared for the first time, inspiring the movie *Cool Runnings*.

1988 American diver Greg Louganis won gold despite hitting his head on the diving board during qualifying rounds.

NEW TEAMS, NEW HOPE

In the 1990s, the Cold War ended and the Soviet Union split up into 15 different countries, while East and West Germany became one nation. The list of Olympic nations and the medal-winning results tables began to look very different.

At the Barcelona Olympics in 1992, South Africa competed for the first time since 1960, after the ending of Apartheid. The new era was symbolized by the women's 10,000-meter race, which was a close-run contest between Derartu Tulu of Ethiopia and white South African athlete Elana Meyer. Tulu took gold, Meyer silver, then the two athletes ran a victory lap together to show the new mood of peace and cooperation.

Derartu Tulu and Elana Meyer celebrate at the end of the 10,000-meter race in Barcelona, Spain, in 1992.

Amazing Olympics

Some Olympic teams are tiny, with just two or three athletes. The biggest teams usually have more than 600 athletes.

Merchandizing

A logo and slogan are designed for each Olympic Games. In the 1990s, these emblems began to appear on lots of merchandise, including hats, T-shirts, and mugs. Companies pay for a license—the right to use the logo on all kinds of different goods. The Atlanta Games in 1996 made a record $50 million from licensing, and since that time the figure has grown.

A branded jacket worn at the 1996 Olympics. At every Games, you can buy items showing the official emblems.

Host Cities

The IOC chooses a new venue nine years before an Olympic Games is due to take place. The countries bidding for the Games make a presentation to convince the IOC to choose them. After some IOC members were found to have taken bribes in 1998, bidding rules have been tightened up.

Canadian Ross Rebagliati, the first Olympic snowboarding champion ever, at the Winter Olympic Games in 1998.

Olympic Facts and Stats

1992 At the Barcelona Olympics, Chinese diver Fu Mingxia won gold at the age of 13. Spanish rowing cox Carlos Front was the youngest competitor, age 11.

1996 Austrian sailor Hubert Raudaschl competed in a record nine Olympic Games.

1996 The giant Olympic stadium torch was lit in Atlanta, Georgia, by world-famous boxer Muhammad Ali.

1998 Snowboarding became an Olympic winter sport for the first time.

HI-TECH, HIGH COST

In the 2000s, the Olympics grew larger, more hi-tech, and more expensive, too. At the Beijing Olympics in 2008, more than 11,000 athletes from 204 nations competed in 302 events. The event cost almost $39.5 billion to stage.

In 2000, the Games went to Sydney, Australia, and in 2004, they returned to Greece, where some events were held at the ancient stadium of Olympia. The Olympic slogan for the Greek Olympics was "Welcome Home." In 2008, the Beijing Games drew the biggest TV audience ever, with an estimated 4.7 billion viewers and an opening ceremony that lasted four hours and featured 15,000 performers. The crowds saw an athlete ignite the giant Olympic torch as he flew across the stadium.

Amazing Olympics!

The Beijing Games began at 8 P.M. on August 8, 2008, because the number 8 is considered lucky in China.

The Olympic rings on Sydney Harbor Bridge, Australia, during the 2000 Olympics.

The Olympic Stadium built for the 2008 Beijing Olympics in China. It was nicknamed the "Bird's Nest" because of its shape.

Running the Games

The Games were now so big that hundreds of thousands of people were needed to keep all the events running smoothly. There had to be a Technology Operations Center manned by experts to control the many thousands of computers and telephone links. The organizers of the Beijing Olympics even used traditional *feng shui* to plan the position of their new stadiums, believing this would help to bring peace and harmony to the Games.

New Tests for Drugs

The IOC cracked down on drug-takers, using hi-tech testing methods to catch cheating athletes. They set up the World Anti-Doping Agency, which began testing Olympic athletes at thousands of sports events away from the Olympic Games themselves. Competitors who tested positive were banned and had their medals taken away.

Olympic Facts and Stats

2000 At the Sydney Games, the Bahamas won the women's 4 x 100-meters relay, the smallest nation ever to win a team gold.

2004 In the Athens Games, a man with an advertisement written on his chest gatecrashed a diving event and jumped from the diving board in a tutu, shouting: "I love you."

2004 Eighteen-year-old American swimmer Michael Phelps won six gold medals and two bronze medals at the Games.

2008 Michael Phelps won another eight gold medals at the Beijing Olympics to become the most successful Summer Games Olympian ever.

The 2012 Summer Olympics and the Paralympics are set to take place in London, UK. The Summer Games will hold 26 sports in venues around London and the rest of the country.

At the closing ceremony of the Beijing Games, in 2008, the Olympic flag was passed from the mayor of Beijing to the mayor of London. Building had already begun to turn part of London into a giant Olympic Park for the Games. The main stadium is designed to hold 80,000 people and is positioned on an island surrounded by water, with bridges leading up to it.

Olympic Venues

Modern Summer Olympic Games have one main stadium, a swimming pool complex, and a selection of other venues where special events such as sailing and rowing take place. In the UK, sailing will be held off the coast of Weymouth, in Dorset. Soccer will be played in stadiums around the country, including Wales and Scotland, and tennis will be held on the world-famous courts in Wimbledon, in southwest London.

Women's boxing will be a new sport at the London Olympics in 2012. This hopeful boxer stands in front of the London logo.

Amazing Olympics

Four thousand trees are to be planted in the London Olympic Park for a green and leafy effect.

The Green Games

Organizers of the London Olympics are aiming to make it the greenest Games yet. The Olympic Park will have gardens to visit, wildlife areas, and thousands of specially planted trees. The organizers will use as much environmentally friendly technology as they can, and expect the stadium and the Olympic Village to be re-used after the Games for homes and events. The cost of the Olympics runs into many billions, but supporters say that its facilities will benefit the country in the long run.

The design for the 377-foot (115-m) high spiral sculpture, the Orbit Tower, at the London Games.

Olympic Facts and Stats

2012 The Olympic torch will travel around the UK before it reaches London. Up to 8,000 people will take part in the torch-carrying relay.

2012 It's thought that up to one in three people worldwide may watch the London Olympic Opening Ceremony on TV.

2012 Women's boxing will be a new Olympic sport in 2012.

2012 There will be a record 5,000 drug tests on athletes at the London Games.

OLYMPIC FUTURE

Olympic Games are planned years into the future. They need lots of organizing, from designing and building the venues to looking after visitors, making deals with sponsors, and choosing designs such as the official logo and poster.

The 2014 Winter Olympics are due to be held in Sochi in Russia, and the 2016 Summer Olympics and Paralympics will take place in Rio De Janeiro, Brazil. These cities are already busy with their preparations and the IOC will be keeping an eye on their progress. Meanwhile, other countries around the world are planning bids to host future Olympics, deciding on the best city to put forward as a location, and creating virtual 3D pictures of how their Games might look.

Olympic Designs

Once a city has been selected, it's time to start organizing the marketing—choosing designs for logos, posters, and even designs for the medals and the outfits judges and referees wear. One of the designs redone for each Games is a set of pictograms—symbols—for each sport used on signs and posters at Olympic venues.

The 2010 Winter Olympics were held in Vancouver, in Canada. The 2014 Olympics will be held at Sochi in Russia.

A London Olympics pictogram. Every sport has one.

A virtual picture of how the Olympic park will look at Rio De Janeiro, Brazil, in 2016.

The Youth Olympics

The newest Olympic event is the Youth Olympics, to be held every four years just like the main Games. Young athletes between the ages of 14 and 18 take part, to experience world-class competition and perhaps go on to appear in the main Olympics in the future. The first Summer Games was staged in Singapore in 2010 and the first Winter Youth Olympics takes place in Innsbruck, Austria, in 2012. The 2014 Summer Youth Olympics will be held in Nanjing in China.

Amazing Olympics

At the Youth Olympics, the judges and officials at the Games are young people, as well as the athletes.

Olympic Facts and Stats

Rio De Janeiro in Brazil will be the first-ever South American city to host an Olympic Games.

No Olympic Games have ever been held in Africa.

India has never hosted the Games, despite having one of the largest populations of any country.

The 2012 Olympics has two official mascots, Wenlock and Mandeville, characters shaped like drops of steel from the Olympic stadium.

GLOSSARY

Amateur athlete Someone who doesn't earn money from their sport, which is not their full-time job.

Apartheid The segregation (separation) of black and white people in South Africa during part of the twentieth century, which led to South Africa being banned from the Olympics.

Archery Shooting at targets using a bow and arrows.

Boycott Refusing to take part in something as a protest.

Broadcasting rights Permission to show the Olympics on TV. Broadcasting companies pay the Olympic organizers for this.

City-states Cities in ancient Greece that governed themselves, with their own laws and customs.

Cold War A period between the 1950s and 1980s when there was suspicion and hostility between the communist countries of the Soviet Union and Western democratic countries of North America and Europe.

Communism A way of organizing a country so that everything is owned by the state and all the profits are shared between the people.

Equestrian An event involving horses.

Feng shui A Chinese belief that objects positioned in a certain way can bring harmony.

IOC International Olympic Committee, the organization that runs the Olympic Games. It is headed by the President of the IOC.

Licensing Selling the rights to companies to put Olympic logos and mottos on their products.

Logo Official badge. Each Olympic Games chooses its own logo.

Marathon A long-distance running race.

Mascot A cartoon character chosen to symbolize an Olympic Games.

Nazi A member of the National Socialist German Workers' Party, which came to power in Germany in 1933 under the leadership of Adolf Hitler.

Olympia The site of the first Olympics, held in ancient Greece in 776 B.C.E.

Olympiad An Olympic event held every four years.

Olympic motto *"Citius, Altius, Fortius"*—Latin for "Higher, Faster, Stronger."

Olympic oath A promise made by athletes and judges to abide by the rules and honor the values and spirit of the Olympic Games.

Olympic rings The logo of the Olympic Games, made up of five rings representing Africa, Asia, the Americas, Europe, and Oceania, on a white background symbolizing peace.

Olympic torch A flame brought from Olympia in Greece to the Olympic stadium in the host city.

Olympic Village Accommodation built for the athletes taking part in the Games.

Pankration A violent combination of boxing and wrestling, which was an event held in the ancient Greek Olympics.

Performance-enhancing drugs Drugs taken to make an athlete perform better (also called "doping").

Pictogram A simple picture used as a symbol.

Professional athlete Someone whose sport is their full-time job, from which they earn money.

Quarantine A period of isolation for a person, animal, or plant, in order to prevent the spread of infection.

Rowing cox The person who steers the boat and helps keep the crew in time with each other.

Sponsor A company that pays to get its products used and displayed at the Olympic Games or elsewhere.

Sprinter A fast runner.

Track and field event An event that takes place on the athletic running track, or in the center of the running track, such as long jump or javelin-throwing.

World Anti-Doping Agency Set up by the International Olympic Committee to test athletes for illegal drug-taking. WADA for short.

Youth Olympics Summer and Winter Olympic Games held every four years for athletes between 14 and 18 years old.

Zeus King of the ancient Greek gods, honored at the ancient Olympic Games.

Modern Summer Olympic Games Timeline

1896 Athens, Greece

1900 Paris, France

1904 St. Louis, Missouri

1908 London, UK

1912 Stockholm, Sweden

1916 Not held because of World War I

1920 Antwerp, Belgium

1924 Paris, France

1928 Amsterdam, Netherlands

1932 Los Angeles, California

1936 Berlin, Germany

1940 Canceled because of World War II

1944 Canceled because of World War II

1948 London, UK

1952 Helsinki, Finland

1956 Melbourne, Australia

1960 Rome, Italy (First Paralympic Summer Games also held)

1964 Tokyo, Japan

1968 Mexico City, Mexico

1972 Munich, West Germany

1976 Montreal, Quebec, Canada

1980 Moscow, USSR

1984 Los Angeles, California

1988 Seoul, South Korea

1992 Barcelona, Spain

1996 Atlanta, Georgia

2000 Sydney, Australia

2004 Athens, Greece

2008 Beijing, China

2012 London, UK

2016 Rio De Janiero, Brazil

Winter Olympics Timeline

1924 Chamonix, France

1928 St. Moritz, Switzerland

1932 Lake Placid, New York

1936 Garmisch, Germany

1940 Canceled because of World War II

1944 Canceled because of World War II

1948 St. Moritz, Switzerland

1952 Oslo, Norway

1956 Cortina d'Ampezzo, Italy

1960 Squaw Valley, California

1964 Innsbruck, Austria

1968 Grenoble, France

1972 Sapporo, Japan

1976 Innsbruck, Austria

1976 First Paralympic Winter Games held Ornskoldsvik, Sweden

1980 Lake Placid, New York

1984 Sarajevo, Yugoslavia (now Bosnia)

1988 Calgary, Alberta, Canada

1992 Albertville, France

1994 Lillehammer, Norway

1998 Nagano, Japan

2002 Salt Lake City, Utah

2006 Turin, Italy

2010 Vancouver, British Columbia, Canada

2014 Sochi, Russia

Useful Olympic web sites

www. olympic.org The official web site of the Olympic Movement.

www.www.teamusa.org Official site of the U.S. Olympic Team.

www.london2012.com The official web site of the London Summer Olympics, 2012.

www.paralympics.org The official web site of the Paralympics.

www.enchantedlearning.com/olympics Find out about the history of the ancient Greek Games and print up a game activity book.

INDEX